# THE LIVES OF MINIBEASTS

# Beautiful BUTTERFLIES

By

# Holly Duhig

©2017
Book Life
King's Lynn
Norfolk PE30 4LS

ISBN: 978-1-78637-186-7

All rights reserved
Printed in Malaysia

Written by:
Holly Duhig

Edited by:
Charlie Ogden

Designed by:
Danielle Jones

A catalogue record for this book
is available from the British Library

## Photo Credits

**Abbreviations: l-left, r-right, b-bottom, t-top, c-centre, m-middle.**

Cover & throughout – Boule, Super Prin, suns07butterfly, Le Do, Eric Isselee, jps, Jausa, mashe, oksana2010, Ian 2010, Feng Yu, Tischenko Irina, Elena Elisseeva, Denise Torres, sakhorn. 2 – grafvision, 4 – Sari ONeal. 5t – Ultrashock 5b – Jubal Harshaw. 6 – Zdenek Kubik. 7 – KULISH VIKTORIIA. 8 – Rosalba Matta Machado. 9 – Anest. 10 – THEJAB. 11 – Mathisa. 12 – Beata Becla. 13 – Grapevine. 14 – Victoria M Gardner. 15 – Protasov AN. 16 – Anettphoto. 17 – Jakub Zak. 18 – IVP. 19 – majeczka. Images are courtesy of Shutterstock.com. With thanks to Getty Images, Thinkstock Photo and iStockphoto. 20main – Sharon Day 20b – studio on line. 21 – Pan Xunbin. 22 – Mayura Ladaeng, Boule, Matee Nuserm, Ken Tannenbaum, Valentyna Chukhlyebova.

# CONTENTS

Words that look like **this** can be found in the glossary on page 24.

# WHAT IS A BUTTERFLY?

Butterflies are insects with six legs and two antennae. They are known for having bright and colourful wings.

A butterfly is a living thing. It needs food and water to live. Its wings help it to fly around and find food.

Antennae

Butterflies use their antennae to smell. They are like two very long noses!

This is what butterfly antennae look like under a magnifying glass.

# WHAT DOES A BUTTERFLY LOOK LIKE?

This is a peacock butterfly. Its wings are red with four spots.

A butterfly has four wings. Different butterflies have different patterns on their wings.

The bodies of butterflies are very long and thin. They have long legs, which they can use to taste leaves. This is how they decide which leaf to lay their eggs on.

The eggs don't fall off because they are very sticky.

Female butterflies lay their eggs on the underside of leaves. This **protects** the eggs from the rain.

A caterpillar hatches from each egg. A caterpillar begins life by eating the leaf that it was hatched on.

Caterpillar

# CRAZY CATERPILLARS

Chrysalis

Caterpillars have long bodies without wings and they spend most of their time eating leaves. When caterpillars have eaten enough leaves, they make themselves a chrysalis.

A chrysalis is a hard shell that keeps the caterpillar safe while it changes into a butterfly. It stays in its chrysalis for about two weeks before **emerging**.

Caterpillar

Chrysalis

Butterfly

# WHERE DO BUTTERFLIES LIVE?

Butterflies live outdoors where there are lots of plants and flowers. They like to live in places with warm weather.

When it rains, butterflies use trees and rocks to protect themselves. You can help butterflies to stay safe when it rains by putting a butterfly house in your garden.

Butterfly House

# WHAT DO BUTTERFLIES EAT?

Proboscis

Butterflies have a long, straw-like tongue called a proboscis. Butterflies use their proboscis to drink the **nectar** in flowers.

Butterflies often drink from puddles because they are not very deep. They also eat fruit when they can find it.

Try putting fruit in your butterfly house to attract butterflies.

# WHAT DO BUTTERFLIES DO?

Butterflies usually only live for two to four weeks. Most of this time is spent trying to find a **mate** so they can lay eggs.

Butterflies' eyes are very good at spotting bright colours, such as the colours on another butterfly's wings. This makes it easier for them to find a mate.

Butterflies are also good at spotting the bright colours of flowers. This helps them find food.

17

# HOW DO BUTTERFLIES HELP?

Pollen

Butterflies help new flowers to grow. When butterflies drink nectar, they collect **pollen** from the flower on their legs.

Butterflies carry this pollen to the next flower they land on. This flower then uses the pollen to make seeds. These seeds then grow into new flowers.

Seeds

# BEAUTIFUL BUTTERFLIES

The Monarch Butterfly

10 cm

The monarch butterfly is a **species** of butterfly that lives in North America. It has a 10 centimetre **wingspan**!

The dead-leaf butterfly looks like an autumn leaf.
This makes it harder for other animals to spot it.

Dead-Leaf Butterfly

# FUN FACTS

Female butterflies usually live for longer and are bigger than the males.

A group of butterflies is called a kaleidoscope (kal-eye-da-scope).

0 1 2 3 4 5 6 7 8 9 10 11 12

Instead of using their tongues, butterflies taste with their feet.

The largest butterfly in the world is the Queen Alexandra's birdwing. This butterfly's wingspan can be over 25cm!

14  15  16  17  18  19  20  21  22  23  24  25  26  27  28  29  30

# GLOSSARY

| | |
|---|---|
| emerging | moving out of something |
| nectar | a sweet liquid made by flowers in order to attract insects |
| pollen | a powder-like substance made by plants |
| protects | looks after or keeps safe |
| species | a group of very similar animals that can produce young together |
| wingspan | the distance between the tips of an animal's wings |

# INDEX